English for Academic Study:

Writing

Teacher's Book

Anne Pallant

University of **Reading**

Centre for
Applied Language Studies

Garnet
EDUCATION

Credits

Published by
Garnet Publishing Ltd.
8 Southern Court
South Street
Reading RG1 4QS, UK

First published 2004
Reprinted with corrections 2004
Second edition published 2006
Reprinted 2008
Fully revised 2009
Reprinted 2009

ISBN: 978 1 85964 502 4

British Cataloguing-in-Publication Data
A catalogue record for this book is available from
the British Library.

Production
Project manager: Simone Davies
Project consultant: Rod Webb
Editorial team: Penny Analytis, Simone Davies,
                      Fiona McGarry, Nicky Platt
Design and layout: Mike Hinks

Printed and bound
in Lebanon by International Press

Contents

Acknowledgements

I would like to acknowledge the important contribution of Ros Richards as the author of a report on the research literature on academic writing. Many of the principles of the course are based on the observations and recommendations in this report. I would also like to thank Ros Richards for her valuable evaluative comments on the early versions of the material.

I would like to thank John Slaght for his collaboration on activities linked to the reading material in the *Reading and Writing Source Book*.

I would also like to acknowledge the many teachers and students at the Centre for Applied Language Studies who have contributed to the process of trialling and evaluating this material, in particular Beverley Fairfax, Mary Ferguson, Helen Fraser, Belinda Hardisty, Clare McClean, Pete McKichan, Jane Short and Sebastian Watkins. I would like to thank Clare McClean for her contribution to Unit 1 of phrases for making polite suggestions for Peer Feedback.

I would also like to thank the teachers and students at the Language Centres of the University of Surrey and Robert Gordon University who have also used this material and given feedback.

The author and publishers would like to thank Ron White for his contributions to some of the questionnaire on pp.11–15, and for the expressions of comparison and contrast, adapted from pp. 6–9 and 68–69, respectively, in Ron White and Don McGovern's *Writing*, Hemel Hempstead: Phoenix ELT (1994).

The task on page 78 is taken from McGovern, Don *Reading*, Hemel Hempstead: Phoenix ELT (1994).

Anne Pallant, Author, May 2009

Book map

Unit	Unit essay	Objectives
1 Academic achievement	Writing an essay: *What are the aims of academic study and how can they be achieved?*	• Reflecting on how to achieve academic success: questionnaire 1.1–1.4 • Reflecting on issues in academic writing: questionnaire 1.5–1.8 • Overcoming difficulties of academic writing: reflecting on issues in writing • Acknowledging expectations of the reader: reflecting on issues in writing • Reflecting on different approaches to organizing ideas: planning and introductions • Evaluating writing
2 Early human development	Writing an essay: *Nature strongly influences early human development. Discuss.*	• Analyzing the essay title • Considering how to organize ideas • Choosing information to support ideas • Practising how to write paragraph leaders
3 Telemedicine	Writing an examination essay: *As technology continues to improve, the range of potential uses of telemedicine will increase. Telemedicine will offer more beneficial applications in preventing disease than in curing disease. Discuss.*	• Understanding differences between writing course work and writing for examinations • Developing rapid analysis of essay questions • Making decisions about organizing ideas • Completing essays within a time limit
4 Statistics without tears	Writing an essay: *Statistics should be interpreted with caution as they can be misleading; they can both lie and tell the truth. Discuss.*	• Organizing ideas in response to an essay title • Identifying useful information in a text • Ending paragraphs with an effective sentence • Writing concluding paragraphs
5 Human activity and climate change	Writing an essay: *What role has human activity played in causing climate change?*	• Writing clear definitions • Supporting and developing ideas
6 The global village	Writing an essay: *Discuss the positive and negative effects of globalization on the world today.*	• Choosing patterns of organization: cause and effect • Incorporating information from research
7 The new linguistic order	Writing an assignment: choice of three titles	• Simulating a real essay assignment: preparation • Looking at other patterns of organization

Introduction

1 Principles and approach

1.1 An integrated approach

At the beginning of the course, it is important to go over the approach with the students so that they understand the rationale that underpins the teaching activities. This introduction to the Teacher's Book relates some of the principles mentioned in the student's introduction to the literature on English for Academic Purposes (EAP) writing (as discussed in Richards, 1999). Explicit links can therefore be made as to why students are asked to engage in certain activities.

A higher-level group can be asked to read through the introduction to the Course Book in their own time, and then given time in class for a plenary discussion of any questions or issues arising. A lower-level group may need a more step-by-step reading of the introduction and you may wish to produce some activities for them to use in conjunction with it.

You will find that students relate more closely to the contents of the introduction after completion of the tasks. You should therefore encourage them to refer to the introduction throughout the course.

EAS Writing was designed so that it can be used as an integrated course with *EAS Reading* in the same series, or as an independent writing course. However, if used as an independent course, the students are still expected to carry out background reading for the writing topics. It is for this reason that the course comes with reading source material (*EAS Reading & Writing Source Book*), which also contains the reading texts from the reading course.

One of the main reasons for supporting an integrated approach to writing is that it responds to the results of research into the development of students' critical thinking skills. By briefly looking at examples of the descriptors of the National Qualifications Framework for higher education, it can be seen how important this aspect of a student's skills development is. The different levels of qualification are Certificate (C), Intermediate (I), Honours (H), Master's (M) and Doctoral (D). The following table gives one example of a descriptor relating to critical thinking for each level.

Level	Example of descriptors relating to critical thinking
C	Students are expected to communicate the results of their study/work accurately and reliably, and with structured and coherent arguments.
I	Students are expected to communicate information, arguments and analysis, in a variety of forms, to specialist and non-specialist audiences, and deploy key techniques of the discipline effectively.
H	Students are expected to evaluate arguments, assumptions, abstract concepts and data (that may be incomplete) critically; to formulate judgements and to frame appropriate questions to achieve a solution – or identify a range of solutions to a problem.
M	Students are expected to deal with complex issues both systematically and creatively, make sound judgements in the absence of complete data, and communicate their conclusions clearly to specialist and non-specialist audiences.
D	Students are expected to make informed judgements on complex issues in specialist fields, often in the absence of complete data, and to be able to communicate their ideas and conclusions clearly and effectively to specialist and non-specialist audiences.

To prepare international students fully for their future study environments, as well as to develop their English language competence, students need to be introduced to the conventions peculiar to academic study in the UK; furthermore, they need training in the skills necessary to function successfully within these conventions, especially in academic writing. Such conventions include critical analysis and argument in extended academic writing. Many students come to study in England from cultural and academic backgrounds where they do not need to be critical of the works of others, nor formulate their own argument with well-founded supporting evidence; they are therefore not fully aware of the level of critical analysis and argument required in academic writing for postgraduate studies in UK universities. Ideally, they require a period of transition in which they are introduced to the new academic culture. EAP teaching material should therefore include tasks and activities that train students to develop their critical thinking skills.

EAP research supports an integrated approach to the teaching of reading and writing. Critical thinking is viewed by Carson as 'the ability to transform information for their own (students') purposes in reading and to synthesize their prior knowledge with another text in writing … . Together, reading and writing facilitate the development of critical thinking' (1993, p.100). Similarly, Belcher defines critical thinking as 'responding in an evaluative, analytical way to texts' (1995, p.135). Grabe & Kaplan assert that the ideal writing course would 'present topical issues and writing tasks which motivate and engage students, while at the same time being challenging and providing opportunities for learning' (1996, p.262). The implications of the research for teaching academic writing are that there should be provision for an integrated skills approach which includes the specific development of critical thinking skills.

1.2 Course structure

Each unit has a writing topic based on the relevant reading text in the Source Book. This follows the principle that students read an academic text for a particular purpose on their academic course. One of the main purposes of the source texts is to provide students with information to support their ideas in their written assignments. They process and critically analyze that information, before incorporating it within their own argument; thus, they engage in a problem-solving activity. It is important to reflect this process on an academic writing programme.

1.3 Task design

The tasks and activities have been designed so that students can develop the different aspects of their writing (as stated in the introduction to the Course Book), and develop effective strategies for approaching a writing task in carefully scaffolded stages. Scaffolding involves breaking down large tasks into smaller ones, with a clear indication of the steps involved in this process, and using questioning techniques to guide students towards task completion. It also involves identifying, teaching, developing and reviewing strategies which students can employ for different types of activities and tasks (Bruner, 1983). This approach reflects the research which suggests that students need to be taught to be more strategically aware of their goals and be given ways to carry out these goals in writing.

Flower and Hayes (1990) assert that recognizing and exploring the rhetorical problem is a teachable process through the development of strategies for appropriate goals. Chamot & O'Malley (1994, p.7) claim research which finds that effective learning relates more to how strategies are used than to the overall number used. They suggest scaffolding techniques for learning these strategies, which are classified into metacognitive (thinking about and evaluating one's learning process), cognitive (interacting with material to be learned) and socio-effective (interacting with another person to assist learning). The fact that writers write differently at different stages of their writing development (Bereiter & Scardamalia, 1987) reinforces the need for scaffolded activities. The practical implications are to teach students how to use strategies to achieve their goals in writing, develop scaffolding techniques, familiarize students with a variety of task and genre types, and describe an explicit route through the teaching materials.

This combined approach, taking into account the process approach, the development of critical thinking in writing, the microskills of writing and the importance of genre, reflects the major emphasis placed by many researchers on the need for a balance between the processes of writing (which are creative, cognitive, communicative) and the demands made by the contexts in which, and for which, writing takes place (Tribble, 1996; Grabe & Kaplan, 1996; Johns, 1993; Leeds (ed.), 1996). An implicit interpretation of this view can be seen in the reviewing, focusing and evaluating phases of the process models; it can be assumed that the writer applies judgement to carry out these processes in the context of her/his understanding of (and feedback on) the particular discourse conventions and social context of the assignment in question. Johns argues that there is 'a natural integration of process and product in academic writing' (1993, p.276).

1.4 The importance of the reader

Research recognizes the strong role of the 'outside reader', when writers make decisions about their approach to a task; Raimes (1991) describes the reader as 'powerful'. This is the person who will read and judge the end product. One of the implications of this research is the consideration that needs to be given to the impact of rhetorically specific wording, that is, analyzing the demands that the task makes upon the reader in terms of how they construct their response. This involves consideration of language use and structural organization. Hence, activities are included in which students carefully analyze the writing task to raise their awareness of these aspects of writing before starting to plan and write.

It is valuable to refer back to the introduction as you work your way through the book with your class, to put an activity into the context of the approach. For example, after doing a peer evaluation session, you could refer back to the section on critical thinking skills and ask the students how they feel their critical thinking has developed after doing the peer evaluation.

2 Using *EAS Writing*

2.1 Pair and group work

Many of the activities on this course require students to participate in a lot of discussion with their classmates, for example, about how they think they should develop an essay structure, or to share their ideas for content. The aim of these discussions and comparisons of answers is for students to heighten their awareness of issues such as: that there is more than one way to approach a problem, that there is no one right answer, and that in carrying out discussion they develop their critical thinking ability. Although it might seem that there is rather a lot of discussion for a writing course, by verbalizing their thoughts, students develop their writing strategies further. This needs to be explained *explicitly* to the students, some of whom may question why they are talking so much in a writing class.

Obviously, the rate at which you complete the activities and work in the book will depend on the level and experience of your class. To some extent this flexibility is built into the Teacher's Book, but you will also need to exercise your judgement as to how long you need to spend on some activities. Some students will find certain tasks very challenging, but usually when encouraged to pursue them, they will see the benefit of having done so – and their writing will improve.

2.2 Multiple drafting

An inevitable result of adopting the process approach is that students will often be working on the first draft of one essay, while revising the previous one to produce a third draft. You will soon get into a pattern of timing and organization, so that neither you nor the students are overwhelmed by the amount of work there is to be done.

2.3 Marking and giving feedback

An effective approach to marking students' second drafts and giving feedback is provided below. By going through these stages of feedback, students markedly improve their writing skills over the period of the course.

A suggested photocopiable feedback form is given at the end of this Introduction which you can use to make comments on specific areas of the writing task:
- *task achievement*, i.e., how the student has responded to the writing task, as stated in the title;
- *organization*, i.e., how effectively the student has organized her/his ideas;
- *language*, i.e., appropriate use of vocabulary and grammar;
- *content*, i.e., relevancy and depth of the content;
- additional comments.

The form provides a record of students' progress, which can be kept in their portfolio. Note that all the photocopiable materials in this book are also available as downloadable files in the teacher's section of the EAS website – www.englishforacademicstudy.com.

2.4 Language feedback

It is recommended that you use symbols to identify language errors, which the students then correct themselves. An example error correction sheet with the key to the symbols is given in photocopiable form at the end of this Introduction. You may prefer to negotiate alternative meaningful symbols with your own students, and adjust the sheet accordingly. For example, with lower-level students, you may prefer to limit the number of symbols they use at the beginning.

You should provide the students with a completed error correction sheet when you return the second draft of their essays. They can then count up the number of errors you have marked in each category and write it on their sheet. They should also be encouraged to write a comment about each category, such as, 'I'll especially check for VF next time,' or 'I'll check the grammar rule for this.'

Students should keep all their essays in a file, as a portfolio, together with the error correction sheet. This will enable them to check their own progress; the students will have a target of reducing the number of errors in each category over the period of the course. It is suggested that you collect the error correction sheet with the third draft of the student essay. This will give you a chance to check they are completing it, and at the same time, make a copy for yourself.

One method of dealing with feedback on the common language errors displayed in students' writing is to identify one sentence in each student's essay that contains a common error. You can type these out, possibly adding the error correction symbols, and give each student a copy for them to study and identify the errors. The identification stage can be done at home or in the class, but it is then useful to follow up with a pair discussion in class followed by a plenary with examples on OHT. You can then discuss different possible ways to correct each sentence, ending up with a satisfactory version on OHT.

This approach:
- develops the students' ability to self-correct language errors;
- fosters students' critical ability;
- helps build students' confidence in their ability to be effective editors of their own work and respond effectively to the use of symbols.

You will undoubtedly find that you will need to do some remedial work on students' language. A summary of the stages in giving feedback is as follows:

1 Take in students' second drafts, along with their plans and first drafts.
2 Bring students' attention to language errors by using symbols on their scripts.
3 Comment on other aspects on the feedback sheet and on the essay (photocopy feedback sheet).
4 Give back essays and feedback sheets, along with the student error correction sheet.
5 Ask students to look at your feedback and ask you any questions that might arise; ask them to complete a student error correction sheet.
6 Ask students to write a third draft, revising and correcting according to your comments.
7 Take in second and third drafts; give feedback on how much revision students have done and improvements; correct any outstanding language errors.

2.5 Timed writing

There are three timed writing activities, which should be completed over the period of the course. The first one, in Unit 3b, is preceded by some activities to raise students' awareness of the process they go through when writing under time pressure. A suggested marking scheme is given on pages 50–51. Two further timed writing activities are given on pages 48 and 49.

2.6 Developing referencing skills using the Source Book

EAS Writing focuses on developing students' ability to write in a clear and concise academic style. Although referencing is an important part of academic writing, this aspect has not been incorporated into the course, as it was felt it would place an extra burden on the students at this stage.

A consequence of this decision is that example extracts from students' work in the Course Book do not contain references to sources. It is therefore important to point out to students that this is simply an indication of the kind of work they will be expected to produce *at this stage* and that at a later stage they will be taught how to incorporate referencing. This could be done using your own material or by making use of another title in the *EAS* series, *Extended Writing & Research Skills*.

However, even at this stage, students need to appreciate the importance of acknowledging sources and begin to notice how it is carried out. They should be made aware that omitting references to sources amounts to theft of intellectual property and that there could be serious repercussions if this happens in genuine pieces of academic writing they will be submitting as part of their future studies.

Should you wish to focus on the development of basic academic writing skills in line with the objectives of *EAS Writing*, you can prepare the students for future referencing in the following two ways:

a) **Recognizing different styles of referencing**
Encourage students to notice that different sources are referenced in different ways. Exposure to and general discussion comparing style, content and intended readership is not only an important study skill, but will also prepare students for referencing their own sources.

The Source Book contains text types from a range of sources, for example:
- serious magazine articles intended for the general reading public or for educational purposes, such as from *The Economist*, *Scientific American* or *Understanding Global Issues*;

- texts taken from more academic sources such as Atkinson R.L. et al.'s Hilgard's Introduction to Psychology, and from an academic journal Foreign Policy, or from a book described as a 'primer for non-mathematicians', *Statistics without tears*.

It is important that the difference in text styles is regularly pointed out to students. For example, in Unit 2, *Early human development*, there are a range of examples of internal referencing (see Source Book page 13, right-hand column). In Unit 5, *Human activity and climate change*, however, the original source is a brochure put together at the request of the UN Environment Programme: World Meteorological Organization and the text has been compiled by a number of academics. As a result, no exact authorship is attributed to any specific contributor in the original document. In such a case, the authorship of any quote or paraphrase from the text is best indicated as Hamburg et al. (updated 2004*) because Steven Hamburg is mentioned first in the alphabetically-arranged list of contributors. It is important for students to appreciate that the origin of this source is very different from other texts in the same Source Book.

Since the original completion of the source materials two of the texts have become available online. These are Human activity and climate change *and* The new linguistic order. *They can be viewed at* http://www.gcrio.org/ipcc/qa/contributors.html *and* http://www.uoc.edu/humfil/articles/eng/fishman/fishman.html *respectively. Students could be encouraged to visit these sites and, in fact, to reference them accordingly in their work.*

b) **Evaluating sources**

Students clearly need to assess the currency of any text they use to fulfil their reading purpose and the credentials of the authors. As much guidance as possible is provided in the Source Book for this purpose (see for examples the bibliographical information supplied about the authors of Acid rain or Skylarks in decline), and there is ample opportunity to explore the credentials and currency of the authors by going beyond the Source Book. For example, although the article *Economics focus: On the move* is not strictly academic, the text *International Migration & The Integration of Labour* (Chiswick & Hatton 2002), referred to in *The Economist* article is very much so. In fact, students can be encouraged to verify this for themselves by viewing the abstract for this text at *ftp://repec.iza.org/RePEc/Discussionpaper/dp559.pdf*, or by utilizing their university library service's online or hardcopy facilities.

Students need to take into consideration the source of any text they use and the original intended readership. At some stage during the teaching of every unit, this should be a general teaching point. The students should consider the relative academic weight that certain texts may carry in comparison with others in the Source Book. In addition teachers should draw students' attention to the fact that a range of texts has been used in the materials in order to develop students' exposure to relatively dense and content-packed texts, in preparation for their future academic studies.

Unit summaries

These provide an opportunity for students to reflect on what they have done at the end of each unit. You may wish the students to complete the unit summaries in class or in their own time. If they complete them out of class, time should be found in class to discuss what the students have done.

Other features

Glossary: This contains a useful list of terms that the students will need to know during the course.
Study tips: These contain additional information that can be used by the students as a ready reference to a range of study issues related to the writing skill.
Web resources: There are suggested web resources at the end of each unit. These provide further areas of practice or study on topics or skills related to the unit.

References

Atkinson, R.L., Atkinson, R.C., Smith, E.E., Bem, D.J., Nolen-Hoeksema, S. & Smith, C.D. (ed.). (1999). *Hilgard's introduction to psychology, 13th edition*, Fort Worth, Pa: Harcourt Brace Jovanovich.
Belcher, D. & Braine G. (eds). (1995). *Academic writing in a second language*, Norwood: Ablex.
Bereiter, C. & Scardamalia M. (1987). *The psychology of written composition*, Hillsdale, NJ: Erlbaum.
Bruner, J.S. (1983). *Child's talk: learning to use language*, Oxford: OUP.
Carson, E.J. & Leki, I. (1993). *Reading in the composition classroom*, Boston: Heinle and Heinle.
Chamot, A. & O'Malley, J. (1994). *The CALLA handbook – implementing the cognitive academic language learning approach*, Reading, MA: Addison-Wesley.
Flower, L., Stein, V., Ackerman, J., Kantz, M.J., McCormick, K. & Peck, W.C. (1990). *Reading to write – exploring a cognitive & social process*, Oxford: OUP.
The Framework for Higher Education Qualifications in England, Wales and Northern Ireland [online], http://www.qaa.ac.uk/academicinfrastructure/FHEQ/EWNI/default.asp
Grabe, W. & Kaplan, B. (1996). *Theory and practice of writing*, London: Longman.
Johns, A. (1993). 'Reading and writing tasks in English for Academic Purposes classes: products, processes, and resources' in Carson, J. & Leki, I. (eds.), *Reading in the composition classroom*, Boston: Heinle and Heinle.
Leeds, B. (ed.). (1996).*Writing in a second language*, London: Longman.
Raimes, A. (1991). 'Out of the woods: emerging traditions in the teaching of English' in TESOL Quarterly Vol. 25, TESOL.
Richards, R. (1999). *An overview of the literature on EAP writing*, (unpublished).
Tribble, C. (1996). *Writing*, Oxford: OUP.

Routes through the materials

As stated above, *EAS Writing* can either be used in combination with *EAS Reading* published in the same series, or as a stand-alone course. The books are designed for international students of English intending to pursue academic study in an English-speaking environment, whose IELTS level is between 5.0 and 7.0. However, much of the material can be adapted for use with less proficient students studying on extended courses.

One of the key principles underpinning the approach taken to academic reading is the idea that it should be purposeful; thus, writing provides a purpose for reading in an academic context. The type of information required to complete the writing task will determine the type of reading needed to extract the relevant information and ideas from the text. Note that writing Focus tasks are indicated in many units of *EAS Reading*.

Below are a number of suggested routes through the course material, depending on the length of the intended course and the number of probable teaching hours required to reach the minimum university entrance level. Each of the routes is based on two 90-minute lessons per week. Bear in mind that the amount of work given to students to be completed outside class time will vary, but inevitably, a certain number of hours will be needed to complete written assignments. Students with a higher level of English language are expected to cover the units more quickly than lower-level students.

Note: The allocation of time does not include time for reading the Source Book material. It is suggested that such reading should take place outside the classroom.

Suggested route for 16-week course

Week	Contact hours	Unit
1	3	Unit 1
2	3	Unit 1
3	3	Unit 2
4	3	Unit 2
5	3	Unit 2
6	3	Unit 3
7	3	Unit 4
8	3	Unit 4
9	3	Unit 4
10	3	Unit 5
11	3	Unit 5
12	3	Unit 5
13	3	Unit 6*
14	3	Unit 6
15	3	Unit 7*
16	3	Unit 7

*It is intended that students are encouraged to take more responsibility for independent study with Units 6 and 7.

Suggested route for 10-week course

Week	Contact hours	Unit
1	3	Unit 1
2	3	Unit 1
3	3	Unit 2
4	3	Unit 2
4	3	Unit 3
5	3	Unit 4
6	3	Unit 4
6	3	Unit 5
7	3	Unit 5
7	3	Unit 6
8	3	Unit 6
9	3	Unit 7
10	3	Unit 7

Suggested route for 8-week course

Week	Contact hours	Unit
1	3	Unit 1
2	3	Unit 2
3	3	Unit 2
4	3	Unit 3
5	3	Unit 4
6	3	Unit 4
7	3	Unit 6
8	3	Unit 6

Suggested route for 5-week course

Week	Contact hours	Unit
1	3	Unit 1
2	3	Unit 2
3	3	Unit 4
4	3	Unit 6
5	3	Unit 7

Note: If you are using both the Reading and Writing books in this series, the same pattern can be followed, except that the parallel unit in the Reading book should be covered before that in the Writing book. For example, students should start with the Task introduction in the Reading book, followed by Unit 1 of the Reading book, followed by Unit 1 of the Writing book.

Photocopiable handout

Feedback on writing tasks

Name: *Date:*

Task: *Teacher:*

Task achievement	
Organization	
Language	
Content	
Additional comments	

Photocopiable

Error correction sheet

Text title:

Error type		Number	Example or comment
WO	word order		
WF	word form		
VOC	vocabulary choice		
VF	verb form		
S/V	subject/verb agreement		
T	tense		
CL	clause construction		
PR	preposition		
AR	article		
U	noun is uncountable		
C	noun is countable		
S/PL	singular or plural change needed		
AV	use active voice		
PV	use passive voice		
–	missing word or words		
R	redundant word(s)		
IR	irrelevant information		
INF	language too informal		
P	punctuation		
PARA	paragraph problem		
SP	spelling mistake		
?	meaning unclear		

1 Academic achievement

This unit will help students:
- think about the aims of academic study, and how to achieve them;
- learn about the different stages of the writing process;
- identify and learn how to cope with difficulties in academic writing;
- learn how to consider the knowledge and expectations of their reader;
- think about different approaches to the organization of their ideas.

Task 1: Thinking about academic success

The questionnaire is designed to stimulate students to think about the aims of academic study and how to achieve them; it will also encourage them to think about their individual experience of academic writing. It should therefore raise students' awareness of some of the critical thinking skills involved in writing in UK higher education.

Some students may find it difficult to think analytically about these aspects and will need extra support. If you have a lower-level group, you can choose to omit some of the more challenging sections, and come back to them later in the course when students' awareness has developed further. Remind students that the aim of the questionnaire is to prompt them to think about the requirements of academic life and there are no right or wrong answers.

Students should complete the questionnaire on their own, but monitor and check that they understand the questions. Students should then discuss their answers in groups; after that they can offer the most interesting points of their discussion to the rest of the class in a plenary.

Questions 1.1, 1.2, 1.6, 1.7, 1.8: These focus on the development of the critical thinking skills that students are expected to have, or develop during their time at university. This is based on research carried out in institutions of higher education in the UK.

Questions 1.3, 1.4, 1.5, 1.9–1.14: These questions focus on academic writing. You may want to explain that surveys carried out among academic departments in British universities suggest that *content*, *organization* and *vocabulary* are considered most important by subject tutors in the academic writing of overseas students. Many tutors will tend to overlook minor errors in grammar, as long as they do not seriously interfere with comprehension. Question 1.4: Emphasize the importance of thinking about the identity of the reader. Point out that a writer should always consider the following:
- Who will my reader(s) be?
- What does my reader already know about the topic?
- What will my reader want to know?
- Why will s/he want to know this?

Question 1.9: You may want to elicit various forms of academic writing which can involve different kinds of communication with a reader. Such communication is not always one-way. For example, replies to academic texts are written in the form of letters, articles and conference papers by people with opposing points of view. You could mention:
- published academic books;
- articles published in academic journals;
- papers given at academic conferences;
- dissertations and unpublished monographs found in libraries;
- essays given by students to tutors.

You could then consider the possible forms of communication that could result from each.

The following suggested answers are guidelines only; students should be encouraged to justify alternative suggestions and thus provoke discussion.

Questions 1.1–1.8

1.1 What is the aim of academic study? (Please tick (✓) one or more.)

	to meet intelligent people
	to ensure having a career or future job
✓	to discover more about theories and certain known facts
	to discuss philosophy
✓	to enjoy learning
	to enable members of society to exchange ideas which are intellectually stimulating
✓	to develop personal growth
✓	to contribute to the social and economic development of society
	to pass examinations
✓	to gain a higher-level degree
	to improve cooperation between different members of world society

1.2 How important is it for you as a student to develop the following characteristics while studying at university? (Tick (✓) H for High importance, M for Medium importance, L for Low importance.)

H	M	L	
	✓		knowing your strengths and weaknesses
✓			thinking about how to develop your abilities further
✓			thinking about how to approach a particular task
✓			using a logical, reasoned approach to study
✓			approaching your subject in depth
✓			being interested in finding things out
			learning how to study
✓			communicating results successfully

1.3 What is academic writing? (Please tick (✓) one or more.)

	a mechanical exercise
	groups of grammatically correct sentences
✓	the clear expression of ideas, knowledge and information
	a form of self-expression
✓	a way of exploring, addressing and expressing academic issues
✓	a way of communicating results or information

1.4 To write well academically, how important are the following? (Tick (✓) H for High importance, M for Medium importance, L for Low importance.)

H	M	L	
✓			reading a lot
	✓		studying grammar
	✓		studying vocabulary
		✓	imitating other writers
✓			writing a lot
✓			inviting others to comment on your writing
✓			going back and thinking again about what you have written
✓			rewriting repeatedly until you are satisfied
	✓		understanding the process of writing
✓			meeting the needs of your reader

1.5 How important do you think the following are when writing academic texts? (Tick (✓) H for High importance, M for Medium importance, L for Low importance.)

H	M	L	
	✓		grammatical correctness
	✓		spelling and punctuation (using full stops and commas, etc.)
✓			an appropriate style
✓			overall organization
	✓		vocabulary
✓			good ideas
✓			good use of sources (appropriate citation, bibliography)
✓			relevance of subject content
✓			response to the task

1.6 In which of the following ways can you support your ideas when writing academic texts?

	using personal anecdotes
✓	using facts
✓	using statistics
✓	using examples
	using the news
✓	using information from books, articles, reports, the Internet
✓	using analogies
✓	using the views and attitudes of others
✓	using research data

1.7 Which of the following contribute to successful academic writing?

✓	presenting information clearly and precisely
✓	analyzing questions and issues clearly and precisely
✓	distinguishing between relevant and irrelevant material
✓	recognizing key assumptions
✓	identifying competing points of view
✓	demonstrating excellent reasoning and problem-solving abilities
✓	adopting a critical stance
✓	understanding the context for which you are writing

1.8 **When persuading your tutors or other members of your academic community that your argument is valid, how important are the following? (Tick (✓) H for High importance, M for Medium importance, L for Low importance.)**

H	M	L	
✓			analyzing questions
	✓		stating facts
✓			reasoning your argument logically from facts
✓			explaining key terms
✓			using language appropriate to a particular subject area
✓			using other points of view to strengthen your argument or research
✓			demonstrating the weaknesses of other people's arguments
✓			acknowledging the limitations of your own argument or research
✓			supporting your argument with examples
✓			frequently summarizing your argument
✓			referring to well-argued conclusions

Questions 1.9–1.14

There are a number of different ways of answering these questions. You may wish to make notes of your own answers in the space provided.

1.9 **Should you always think of academic writing as communicating with another person? Why/Why not?**

_____

_____

_____

_____

_____

1.10   **What do you do, or what do you concentrate on, when you are given a writing task:**
a) while you are still writing your first draft?

_____

_____

_____

_____

_____

b) when you have finished your first draft?

_____

_____

_____

_____

_____

c) before you hand in your final draft?

_____

_____

_____

_____

_____

1.11   **What type of academic writing have you done in the past?**

_____

_____

_____

_____

_____

1.12   **What difficulties do you have with writing in English or in your own language?**

_____

_____

_____

_____

_____

1.13 **What do you do when you have difficulties?**

_____

_____

_____

_____

_____

1.14 **Do you enjoy academic writing? Why/Why not?**

_____

_____

_____

_____

_____

Text 1   Academic achievement

Task 2: Microskills: Planning

As preparation for writing, tell the students to read Texts 1-1, 1-2 and 1-3 in the Source Book (pages 7–11, entitled _The influence of class size on academic achievement_ and _The Asian paradox_), and identify information relevant to their essay:

What are the aims of academic study and how can they be achieved?

Content for this title can be generated from both the questionnaire and the reading texts. Content should be discussed in plenary in order that all students have a focus.

Another possible title for which students can generate more information from the reading text is 'Class size is a major factor in contributing to academic success. Discuss.'

2.1 This is a good opportunity to raise students' awareness of the importance of analyzing essay questions (for both examinations and course assignments) to understand what the examiners/lecturers require in the answer. In this question, the key ideas are:
- aims
- academic study
- achieved

You may need to explain the word _aims_.

2.3 If students are having difficulties, refer them back to the questionnaire. Question 1.1 deals with the aims and the other questions deal with ways to achieve the aims.

2.4 Some students may need help with the planning stage. They need to be made aware of how important this is from the start of the course. Emphasize that, if they spend time planning carefully from the beginning, they can save a lot of time later. It may be useful for some groups to see a model of a good plan, with both the paragraphs and the main ideas within the paragraphs easily identifiable. See the example of one way of producing a plan on page 30. You may like to put this on an OHT and build up the paragraph topics with the students, or you may like to give each student a copy, which they complete for their own essay. You should also elicit other possible ways of planning.

2.5 Although it is early on in the course, students should be able to answer the five questions designed to evaluate the plan. However, you may need to run through them, prompting students what to look for. Remind students of the benefits of another person looking at their plans, i.e., if the plan is clear to another person, then the writer has successfully thought about the logical organization and content of their essay.

2.6 Students reflect on the comments on their plans and make changes to them.

2.7 Students begin to write their essays. Point out that at this stage they will be expected to write between 400 and 600 words. However, by the end of the course they should be writing 1,000 words.

2.8 Peer evaluation
According to the progress of your particular group, you will need to decide whether to do the peer evaluation before or after you cover the microskills section on introductions. The advantage of doing it afterwards is that the students will be much more aware of what makes a good introduction and so will be able fully to evaluate their partner's work.

As this is the first peer evaluation session of the course, it is important that an atmosphere of cooperation is established. You should emphasize the positive aspects of evaluation and constructive criticism, as well as the fact that the evaluator is only making suggestions, that the writer may, or may not, choose to implement. However, the writer also needs to understand that the reader's viewpoint is very *valuable*. The writer knows exactly what s/he is writing about, but may omit the necessary links that a reader needs to understand the development of the writer's ideas.

It can be helpful to remind students of the importance of expressing their views in a 'non-threatening' way, by using suitable language. You could point out the difference between the following two examples:
- *You can't/shouldn't do/write that …*
- *It might be easier for the reader to understand this idea if you added more information about …*

Guide students through the selection of suitable phrases for making polite suggestions in the Course Book, page 17.

Some students can be resistant to the idea of peer evaluation, believing that only the teacher can comment on their work. However, if they are made aware of the benefits of this stage in the writing process more explicitly, then the idea becomes more acceptable and relevant to them. The major benefit is that they are being trained to be more critical of the written word, and this eventually affects how they approach their own writing, enabling them to evaluate their essays from a reader's point of view more quickly and efficiently. Remind them that you will not be with them once they start their academic course, and that they need to depend on themselves and their friends, not on you. Also explain that peer evaluation has been shown to train students to be effective evaluators of their writing, and to contribute to the development of critical thinking skills.

You need to decide if, and how much, you want to intervene in the peer evaluation process, as you circulate and monitor the students. In the early stages of the course some students will need guidance from you, and others will want confirmation about one or two points. It is important for them to build up their confidence in their ability to analyze the effectiveness of their peers' writing.

If you do have a student who finds it difficult to evaluate, put her/him into a group of three. Each person will then receive some feedback, as two students will have evaluated each piece of writing. It would be better if the pairs were of mixed nationality, as speakers of the same language tend to organize their writing in a similar way and make similar language errors; there is, therefore, a danger of reinforcement of errors! However, it is not always possible to get this mix, and other factors are relevant too, such as level and ability.

For each essay that the students write, there is a peer evaluation sheet with very specific questions that they should respond to. The main reason for this is that students will find this stage difficult at first, and will not be able to focus and be critical about all aspects of writing. The development of this skill is therefore carefully staged, so that the students gradually build up their ability to evaluate writing. As well as referring to overall structure and general points, the questions will relate to the *microskills* that are being taught in the class. So, for example, if you have been looking at paragraph leaders, then the next peer evaluation will include questions like *Can you identify the paragraph leader in each paragraph?*

You may find that some students want to correct the language in the essays they are peer evaluating. To avoid *inappropriate* correction, you may want to tell them that you, as the language expert, will look at language issues when you see their second drafts.

The first peer evaluation sheet requires students to consider the overall structure of an academic essay and the clarity of ideas. The questions anticipate remedial or revision work on what makes a good introduction and conclusion, and the importance of paragraphing. You will need to decide how much you want to anticipate this, and how much discussion you want to encourage, according to the needs of your group.

The time given to peer evaluation can vary according to the level of the class. Initially, allow *at least* 45 minutes, as students need time to read the essay and then answer the questions. As the question sheets become more detailed, and the essays longer, an hour might be needed, even with a very good group.

You might want to end the session, in plenary, going round the class, quickly asking each student what they are going to change in their draft. The fact that they actually have some concrete changes to make helps to show the usefulness of the session.

PEER EVALUATION: Unit 1

Notes on questions:

1.1 Introduction

a) The students should be able to identify whether the essay has an introduction.

b) You may want to suggest that the introduction should mention the 'key ideas' in the title and explain how the writer is going to approach the topic.

c) Students who are new to this process will have difficulty in making suggestions for improvement. You may want to prompt here.

1.2 Paragraphing

a/b) You may want to remind students that each paragraph should contain a main idea, which is then developed in the paragraph. You may want to discuss the benefits of a logical order of ideas.

c) This question is asking students to decide whether there is enough detailed explanation of the ideas, or examples to illustrate the point. This anticipates future teaching sessions, in later units, on exemplification and development of ideas.

If you feel the need to be more explicit about the development of ideas in a paragraph, you might build up an example on the board or on an OHT. For example, put up the following sentence on the board:

> ***Learning English is useful.***

Then ask the students how they could develop the idea. Emphasize that if this idea is not developed, the reader will be asking her/himself questions like:

> ***Why*** *is it useful? or* ***How*** *is it useful? or* ***Who*** *is it useful for?*

This should elicit answers similar to the following:

It is useful because a knowledge of English enables people to access more information. For example, scientists need to be able to read research articles and books written in English to keep up-to-date in their field. A knowledge of English is also useful for international communication, as it is the most widely spoken language.

Encourage students to ask the questions *How? Why? When? For whom?* about every statement they write. This should help them increase their awareness of the need to develop their ideas in their writing, as well as foster a critical approach to their studies.

1.3 Conclusion

Some students will not have ideas about what makes a suitable conclusion. You may want to explain briefly that the main ideas should be referred to in the conclusion and that it could:
- be a summary;
- draw conclusions;
- look to the future.

This anticipates a future teaching session on writing conclusions.

1.4 Additional information

This question involves students assessing and evaluating the text they have read with the purpose of identifying relevant information to add to their essays. Some students may find this difficult, so it would be a good idea to have a plenary discussion on this and remind students of the importance of continually revising their drafts and including new ideas.

Task 3: Microskills: Introductions

3.1 This is a quick brainstorming activity to elicit students' prior knowledge. Put students in pairs or groups to discuss their ideas, and emphasize that it is also important to say why they have chosen their points.

Have a plenary discussion and write students' ideas on the board. The purpose of this exercise is to help students clarify the important points of the plenary discussion. If you feel your class does not need this step, then leave it and go to Ex 3.4.

3.3 Read through the summary about introductions, and emphasize that throughout the course they will be developing their awareness of what makes a good introduction. However, point out that it is a good idea at the beginning to have a structure to follow.

3.4 In doing this exercise, students should begin to think of a *general* to *specific* pattern of organization for an introduction.

Answers:

a) The order should be: 3, 1, 5, 2, 4.

c) This pattern consists of:

3	a general statement about the topic;
1	general information about the topic relevant to this particular essay;
5/2/4	thesis statement which narrows the topic from general information to a specific viewpoint, which states the controlling ideas of the essay and states also the intention of the writer.

The functions of the sentences are as follows:

3	to introduce the readers to the general topic;
1	to give the reader more general information about the topic related to this essay;
5	to introduce the specific topic with a thesis statement;
2	to state the writer's intent;
4	to extend the statement of the writer's intent.

If you feel that your class needs extra work on what makes a good thesis statement, before doing Ex 3.5, you can do the supplementary exercises which follow. When discussing the thesis statement, you could elicit other suitable verbs to follow 'This essay ...', such as *discuss*, *consider* and *explain*.

Supplementary task: Thesis statements

Copy the thesis statement sheet on page 31 onto an OHT and go through the points with your students.

The ideas are adapted from Reid, J. M., (1988). *The process of composition*, New Jersey: Prentice Hall.

Then ask your students to identify the controlling ideas in the following statements. Ask them how they think the rest of the essay will be developed.

a) In South Africa the AIDS epidemic is beyond human control.

b) Darwin's discovery of evolution has caused much controversy.

c) There are many reasons why international students decide to go abroad to study.

Ask your students to continue each statement with a sentence beginning 'This essay will …'

Students will get further practice in writing thesis statements in Ex 3.6.

Note: This may seem slightly prescriptive, but it has been shown that students find it useful at the beginning to adopt a formulaic approach which they can break away from later when they have acquired a greater awareness of the requirements of academic writing.

3.5 Give students time to look at these introductions individually. Then put them in pairs or groups to discuss their ideas. Have a plenary to emphasize the useful and interesting points.

There is no definite and specific answer to this exercise of evaluating the introductions. However, the following notes may be useful. (Do not worry about language errors at this point.)

Introduction 1
This introduction contains a good example of the general to the specific pattern. However, there is too big a jump in topic from the first three sentences, which deal with education, to the last sentence, which suddenly mentions academic success. So the writer either has to fill the gap between sentence 3 and sentence 4, or change the emphasis of the first three sentences.

Introduction 2
This is fairly successful (apart from some language peculiarities). It could be argued that the first sentence is too specific and should be more general.

Introduction 3
Again, this is quite successful. It would be useful to comment on the first sentence and ask students if it is acceptable to say 'everybody'. Ask them how they would change it. It could be argued that the writer should have made the last sentence more specific by adding '… the related factors which contribute to these two stages of academic success.' This would add more cohesion to the introduction.

Note: This may be an appropriate point to mention something about formal style. Ask students if they think the style is appropriate in this introduction. They should come up with 'our' as being inappropriate here. You could then discuss alternative expressions. Tell them that the use of 'we' and 'I' is traditionally not acceptable in academic writing; it is, however, often used in science and scientific journals when writing up experiments, and increasingly in subjects like sociology, art history, etc., where a personal response is being asked for.

Introduction 4

Although this has a good general to specific pattern, the links between the ideas in the sentences need to be more explicit. For example, sentence 2 should have more explanation about what is 'potential livelihood' and how it can be realized, with some link to the idea in the first sentence. The last sentence shows that the writer is 'off topic'.

Introduction 5

This is included as an example of an introduction which requires much revision. Students should pick up on the first sentence as being inappropriately stated as a question. There is too much detail, which is confused, as the links between ideas are not explicit. There is also a style problem, with some informal language, such as, 'There is good reason to say so' and use of 'I'.

If you feel it is appropriate, for higher-level students a good homework task might be to rewrite one of the introductions, both in terms of content and style.

3.6 Emphasize to the students that they do not need to write the whole essay.

If you feel your students are not ready to write individually, they could do the first introduction in pairs, students could put the introductions on an OHT and the class could evaluate them.

3.7 Students should now have the confidence to revise the introductions of their first essay.

Note: The five introductions are edited versions of authentic student material. This means that grammatical mistakes have been corrected and other changes made where considered appropriate.

Unit summary

You may want the students to complete the unit summaries in class or in their own time. If they complete them out of class, feedback can take place during class time.

You may wish to set up some of the activities, either to clarify what to do, or to help get students thinking about the topics.

Some of the items can be done individually and others are best done in pairs or groups. When working outside the classroom, encourage students to find the time to meet with others and complete any pair or group activities.

The students can complete all three activities without any class preparation. However it would be very useful to discuss their answers to Ex 3 when complete.

1   This activity provides scaffolding for Ex 2.

Answers:
a) brainstorming
b) organizing ideas
c) adopting a critical stance
d) drafting
e) peer feedback

Web resources

CAPLITS: Centre for Academic and Professional Literacies: How to start writing
This site has a diagram of the writing process, showing the stages from pre-writing to proofreading. Students can click on each stage to find more information about it. Other sections of the website include: structure, coherence, cohesion and avoiding plagiarism.
http://caplitswritingcentre.ioe.ac.uk/index.html

Writing machine – Topic, titles and introductions
A section of Hong Kong University's 'writing machine' site that gives tips for writing introductions, looks at different functions of example introductions and has tasks to help analyze and practise writing them.
http://ec.hku.hk/writingmachine/bin2/default.htm

How to plan an essay

TITLE: _____

Introduction

Thesis statement: _____

Paragraph 1

Main idea: _____

Supporting idea 1: _____
Examples: _____

Supporting idea 2: _____
Examples: _____

Supporting idea 3: _____
Examples: _____

Paragraph 2

Main idea: _____

Supporting idea 1: _____
Examples: _____

Supporting idea 2: _____
Examples: _____

Supporting idea 3: _____
Examples: _____

Paragraph 3

_____

_____

Conclusion

_____

_____

Thesis statements

1 The thesis statement is probably the strongest statement in the essay.

2 The thesis statement will probably come at the beginning of the essay, usually at the end of the introductory paragraph.

3 A statement of fact, e.g., *Britain has three major political parties*, does not make a good thesis statement, as it does not provide the opportunity for extensive further development.

4 A question, e.g., *How does the British political system function?* is not a good way to express the thesis. However, the answer to the question is the thesis. *The main aim of academic study is to develop an enquiring mind.*

5 The thesis statement will contain controlling ideas that will be further developed in the paragraphs of the main body of the essay.

6 The thesis statement will be specific.

The ideas are adapted from Reid, J. M. (1988).
The process of composition, New Jersey: Prentice Hall.

English for academic study

2 Early human development

This unit will help students:
- make decisions about what the essay title is asking them to write about;
- consider the most appropriate way of organizing their ideas;
- decide what information in a text is useful to support their ideas;
- practise writing paragraph leaders.

This unit will prepare the students to write an essay on the following topic:
Nurture strongly influences early human development. Discuss.

This unit deals in varying degrees of detail with a number of skills. Some of them will complement other academic skills work, e.g., summarizing information from a text and using this to support ideas, citing correctly; others will be recycled in later units. Higher-level groups should be able to deal with all of them. Lower-level groups need to go into more depth in some skills than others, as indicated in the teacher's notes associated with each activity.

Text 2   Early human development

Task 1: Microskills: Organizing your ideas

1.1 Give students between three and five minutes to do this task. It gives further practice in analyzing essay titles.

1.2 You could have a quick class discussion (five minutes) to confirm ideas. In fact, all the words in the title are key words.

Content for this title can be generated from both the questionnaire and the reading texts. Content should be discussed in plenary in order that all students have a focus.

Another possible title for which students can generate more information from the reading text is 'Class size is a major factor in contributing to academic success. Discuss.'

1.3 Remind students that this should be a flow of all ideas connected with the topic, and the ideas do not have to be organized.

1.4 Place students into groups of three. The aim of this activity is to stimulate students to process further their ideas about the demands of the title and to think about the direction of the essay.

1.5 The aim of this activity is to help students understand the demands of the title in a more explicit way. As students have already brainstormed and discussed the topic, it should be easier for them to make a decision.

If you have a good group, you may feel you can omit this activity, or do it very quickly. If you have a weaker group or a group with less mature students who find this activity challenging, an alternative way to arrive at the same point would be as follows:

Ask them the difference between the following two essay titles:

a) *Nurture strongly influences early human development. Discuss.*
b) *Does nurture influence early human development more than nature?*

They should come up with ideas like:

a) is asking the writer to focus on nurture and to examine the degree to which nurture influences early human development, but also to acknowledge that there are other influences – such as nature – which need to be addressed in the essay.

b) is asking the writer to examine the influence of both nature and nurture and to argue that one is a stronger influence.

If your students are still having difficulty understanding the requirements of the title, present the following title, to which they should be able to relate:

English food strongly influences the extent to which overseas students in England adjust to their new environment.

They should be able to say that the writer of this topic should examine how a dislike of English food can affect the happiness and adjustment of newly-arrived overseas students. They should also be able to say that there are likely to be other factors that influence students' adjustment, such as the weather, accommodation and whether they make friends. They should then be able to transfer this approach to that of the essay for this unit.

1.6 The most appropriate answer is d). However, point out that the influences could have equal strength (as modern psychologists believe, according to the text). The main point is that it is not a purely descriptive essay, but requires a discursive approach and an evaluation of the strengths of the influences, possibly with an argument that one is stronger than the others.

Draw attention to the word *discuss*. If necessary, explain that an essay title can be divided into two parts:

- the words that tell you what to do, e.g., *discuss*, *examine*;
- the words that refer to the subject or content of the essay.

For their purposes in this essay, the word *discuss* should indicate to the students that they should identify the various views on what influences early human development. They should evaluate the strengths of each, with a view to agreeing or disagreeing with the statement in the title.

1.7 This activity introduces the idea that there are different rhetorical patterns in writing and some may be more suitable than others for a particular topic. Weaker students may find this concept difficult, so you may want to move quickly on to the pair or group discussion. The pattern can depend on the emphasis demanded by the essay title. For example, here the first section of the essay might discuss the different possible influences on early human development, then the extent of the influence, and a discussion of the strong influences, focusing on nurture.

Elicit ideas and write them on the board. As this is a discursive essay, the better students would be expected to come up with something like:

- a statement of the number and the labels of the different influences;
- a paragraph or two on each one, which explain how the influence occurs, with some examples and also an account of the researchers and their work;
- an evaluation of the theories/influences. You may want to elicit from them what might be an appropriate order. If they agree with the statement, then they would write about nature first, and then counter-argue with their arguments on nurture.

This will also provide scaffolding for weaker students. However, point out that there is never only one way of approaching an essay title, and that different approaches will be looked at during the course. They will then be in a position to make evaluative decisions as to the most effective approach to take towards their writing.

Note: If you find that your students are having difficulty coping with the whole essay, they can work at paragraph level rather than whole-essay level. Having decided what would be suitable topics for their paragraphs, students can work on one paragraph at a time, building their skills of how to develop an idea in a paragraph in a more gradual way.

1.8 This reading activity aims to develop the students' skills in using information from texts to support their ideas.

Ask students to refer to Texts 2-1, 2-2 and 2-3 in the Source Book (pages 12–15, entitled *Early human development*) and identify useful information to support the points they want to make in their essay. Note that Text 2-1 and some of Text 2-2 contain the most relevant information.

1.9 After they have discussed this in pairs, you may feel you need a plenary to share viewpoints. One way to do this would be to put the text on to an OHT and mark the relevant parts; the weaker students could then mark their own texts.

When students incorporate information in this way, there is a possibility that they will copy from the original text. This would therefore be an appropriate time to remind them that they should summarize the information in their own words, and acknowledge their source. Otherwise, they can be accused of plagiarism.

Supplementary task: Paraphrasing

The students will need further practice in putting information from the text that they want to use for their essay into their own words. There will be some work on expressing other writers' ideas in the students' own words, and summary work, later in this course. However, as students will find it useful to have some practice at this point, the following activities on paraphrasing have been included in the teaching notes.

1 Elicit and write on the board ways students can introduce ideas from other texts to support their writing. These might include (see also photocopiable handout page 40):

> *As Kagan (1979) points out/pointed out, ...*
> *According to Kagan (1979), ...*
> *Research carried out by Kagan (1979) shows/suggests that ...*
> *Kagan (1979) argues/argued that ...*
> *Kagan (1979) has drawn attention to the fact that ...*
> *In an article by Kagan (1979), ...*
> *A study by Kagan (1979) indicates/indicated that ...*
> *Kagan (1979) claims/claimed that ...*
> *Kagan (1979) has expressed a similar view ...*

2 This activity involves the students putting two parts of the text into their own words. You could build up the first one together using OHTs, then ask students to do the second one individually and then compare in twos or threes.

Tell the students to imagine that they have chosen lines 10–16 of the text to support their ideas in their essay.

... Locke believed that the mind of a newborn infant is a "blank slate" (tabula rasa). What gets written on this slate is what the baby experiences – what he or she sees, hears, tastes, smells and feels. According to Locke, all knowledge comes to us through our senses. It is provided by experience; no knowledge or ideas are built in.

Tell the students that their version should contain exactly the same idea as the original, but without using the original words or sentence structure. Elicit ways of doing this.

A suggested approach to this difficult skill is that students identify the words which reflect the key ideas in the text, and then find appropriate alternative words. Ask students to circle the key words in the text, then write them on an OHT and elicit alternative words. You might get something like this:

mind	=	thinking mechanism/brain
newborn	=	new baby
blank slate	=	empty/without content
written	=	established/added
experiences	=	gains
sees, tastes, smells and feels	=	senses
knowledge	=	expertise
ideas	=	thoughts
built in	=	already established/ imprinted

Ask the students to put this information into one or two grammatically accurate sentences. Elicit possible versions and write them on an OHT. Then discuss the different versions and decide which were successful and why.

One possibility is (see also photocopiable handout page 41):

According to Locke (1690), the 17th-century philosopher, a new baby's brain has nothing, neither thoughts nor expertise, established in its thinking mechanism until s/he begins to gain them through the use of her/his senses. Thus, he supports the idea of nurture influencing early human behaviour.

3   Now ask the students to go through the same steps with the following lines (or ones of your own choice) from the text:

Today, most psychologists agree not only that both nature and nurture play important roles but that they interact continuously to guide development. (lines 37–39)

Students do this individually, compare their work in pairs, and then have a plenary to discuss the success of a few versions.

Possible suggestions are:

most psychologists	= the majority of psychologists
agree	= concur
important roles	= essential parts
interact	= work together
continuously	= endlessly/all the time
guide	= lead/bring on
development	= growth

So you might get (see also photocopiable handout page 41):
The majority of modern psychologists concur that nature and nurture play an essential part in the early growth stages, and that they are working together all the time.

Point out that words like *nurture* and *nature* do not need to be changed, as they are key words of the topic.

1.10 Remind students of the value of planning their writing carefully. If they have most of their ideas down on paper in an appropriate order, and an indication of how their ideas will be supported and developed, then it makes the writing of their essays more efficient. Encourage them to use a sheet of A4 paper so that it is easier for them to add ideas and annotate their notes.

It may be useful for some groups to see a model of a good plan, if you feel they are struggling with this activity. See photocopiable handout on page 42 for an example of a partially completed plan for this essay. Students could either complete it individually or in pairs, or could develop their own according to the ideas that they have developed. Emphasize that this plan is only one of many possible approaches.

1.11 Remind students that if someone else cannot understand their plan and has to ask lots of questions, then it needs revising.

1.12 Encourage students to make appropriate changes to their plans.

1.14 You may need to make a decision about whether students do the peer evaluation after doing the work that follows on paragraph leaders in Task 2, as this is a focus of the peer evaluation sheet.

If you have a lower-level group, you may feel that it is appropriate to focus more on specific questions on content, such as:
• What is the topic of each paragraph?
• Are the paragraph topics relevant to the title of the essay?

Task 2: Microskills: Paragraph leaders

2.1 The aim of this activity is to identify the important ideas in a sentence. Refer the students to Texts 2-1, 2-2 and 2-3 in the Source Book.

2.2 The aim of this activity is to raise further awareness, through discussion, of how to identify key ideas in a sentence, and how a good writer can help her/his readers by guiding them as to what comes next in the text. Higher-level students should reach agreement quite quickly, whereas lower-level students will need more time.

2.3 **a)** Ask students to read the paragraphs following these sentences in the text (paragraphs F, G and H), to see if they have decided correctly.

Paragraph F: This introduces the idea that children go through the same stages of motor development, but that experience may contribute to the fact that children go through the stages at a different rate. It therefore does follow the key ideas in the first sentence.

Paragraph G: This is more tricky to explain, as the first sentence is a continuation of the previous paragraph. However, paragraph G does continue with examples of research on how extra stimulation can speed up motor development, as indicated in the first sentence of the paragraph: 'more recent studies indicate that practice … to some extent.'

Paragraph H: This discusses the idea that when children are encouraged and stimulated to speak, the development of speech is accelerated. It therefore does follow the key ideas in the first sentence.

b) Students should be making suggestions like 'they predict/anticipate/control the ideas that follow'.

c) Have a quick class discussion about whether the students predicted the contents of the paragraph correctly.

2.4 Discuss the short paragraph about paragraph leaders. As well as indicating the topic of the paragraph, the paragraph leader acts as a cohesive device, linking the ideas of the essay with the title and with previous and subsequent ideas. Thus, a paragraph leader could be:
a) a *topic sentence* that anticipates the main ideas of the paragraph;
b) a statistic or fact that stimulates discussion about its truth and the evidence;
c) a quotation from a source that stimulates discussion.

Task 2 obviously emphasizes a) a topic sentence; this would be adequate for discussion with lower-level students. If you have higher-level students, you may wish to engage in a wider discussion of possible options for *paragraph leaders*.

Stress the importance of writers helping their readers as much as possible, and that having a clear topic sentence in each paragraph is one way of doing this.

2.5 This activity (and Ex 2.7) gives the students practice in deciding what makes a suitable paragraph leader.

Answers:
a) indicates a paragraph about how useful e-mail is in the office
b) indicates a paragraph about only one use of e-mail (efficient communication with colleagues abroad)
c) is the correct answer, as it indicates a discussion of the uses of e-mail

2.6 The aim of this discussion is for students to clarify their ideas and reach agreement. Encourage students to explain the reason for their choice and say why they did not choose another option. This further develops their critical thinking.

2.7 **Answers:**
a) indicates a paragraph about the reasons why studying in England is useful
b) is the correct answer as it indicates a paragraph about the benefits of studying in England
c) indicates a paragraph about why students prefer to study in England

2.8 See notes for Ex 2.6. At this stage you might want to point out an example of an unsuitable paragraph leader: in paragraph D, the reader is led to believe that the paragraph will be about the effect of environmental events on development, but in fact it is about the genetic programming of development. The effect of the environment is explained in paragraph E, which begins *For example*.

2.9 This activity gives students practice in writing paragraph leaders. Ask the students to read the paragraphs and write suitable paragraph leaders. The paragraph leader should contain similar ideas to the following:

a) Fluency in English offers students many more job opportunities once they return to their own countries, having obtained their degrees.

b) The suggested solutions to the traffic problem should be evaluated in order to establish how viable each of them is.

2.10 Students should now have the confidence to include paragraph leaders in their essay on *Early human development*. If they are about to write their second draft, they should be encouraged to revise their paragraph leaders in the light of the above activities.

Unit summary

1   Although much of this table is easy to complete, the students will nevertheless have to think carefully about some aspects. Encourage them to see this as an opportunity to reflect on what they have done and prepare for Ex 2.

Answers:
1.1–1.6, 1.7, 1.8–1.9, 1.10–1.12, Task 2

2   **Answers:**
   a) key words
   b) relevant
   c) discuss
   d) develop, academic evidence
   e) group, ideas
   f) general statements
   g) plan, first draft
   h) paragraph leaders

Web resources

UEfAP: Academic writing: Organizing the essay
This section of the UEfAP study guide shows different ways of organizing ideas in essays according to function. It also links different essay-types to key words. Once accessed, students should click on *organization*.
http://www.uefap.com/writing/writfram.htm

Language and learning online: What makes a good essay?
A sample essay on the topic of population growth, with commentary that explains how it is organized and gives useful tips on what to include in an essay.
http://www.monash.edu.au/lls/llonline/writing/general/essay/1.xml

Unexplained mysteries
This online community debating forum currently has a formal nature/nurture debate. At some point this forum will be withdrawn.
http://www.unexplained-mysteries.com/forum/index.php?showtopic=60571

Ways of paraphrasing

As Kagan (1979) points out/pointed out, ...

According to Kagan (1979), ...

Research carried out by Kagan (1979) shows/suggests that ...

Kagan (1979) argues/argued that ...

Kagan (1979) has drawn attention to the fact that ...

In an article by Kagan (1979), ...

A study by Kagan (1979) indicates/indicated that ...

Kagan (1979) claims/claimed that ...

Kagan (1979) has expressed a similar view ...

Photocopiable

Photocopiable handout

According to Locke (1690), the 17th-century philosopher, a new baby's brain has nothing, neither thoughts nor expertise, established in its thinking mechanism until s/he begins to gain them through the use of her/his senses. Thus, he supports the idea of nurture influencing early human behaviour.

The majority of modern psychologists concur that nature and nurture play an essential part in the early growth stages, and that they are working together all the time.

Photocopiable

Example of an essay plan for Unit 2

TITLE: NURTURE STRONGLY INFLUENCES EARLY HUMAN DEVELOPMENT. DISCUSS.

INTRODUCTION:

Thesis statement: *General about early human development: researchers have been arguing for many centuries about whether nature or nurture has the stronger influence on early human development. Definitions of nature and nurture. This essay will examine the degree to which nurture influences early human development.*

PARAGRAPH ONE

Main idea: *Strong influence of nurture*

Supporting idea 1: *Locke 17th century*
Examples: *taste, smell*

Supporting idea 2: *Watson and Skinner 1930*
Examples: _____

Supporting idea 3: *Zelazo and Zelazo and Kolb*
Examples: *practice–motor development*

Supporting idea 4: *Kagan*
Examples: *speech level stimulation*

PARAGRAPH TWO

Main idea: *Strong influence of nature*

Supporting idea 1: _____
Examples: _____

Supporting idea 2: _____
Examples: _____

Supporting idea 3: _____
Examples: _____

PARAGRAPH THREE

_____

CONCLUSION:

_____

_____

3b Telemedicine

This unit will help students:
- understand the differences between writing an essay in examinations and writing a course assignment;
- learn how to analyze the essay question quickly;
- make decisions about the most appropriate ways to organize their ideas;
- complete an essay within a time limit.

This unit will prepare the students to write a timed essay on the following topic:
As technology continues to improve, the range of potential uses of telemedicine will increase. Telemedicine will offer more beneficial applications in preventing disease than in curing disease. Discuss.

Task 1: Microskills: Writing in examinations

1.1 The aim of this activity, and Ex 1.2, is to encourage students to think about the process they go through in answering examination questions.

1.2 Students discuss their ideas with another student.

1.4 When students have discussed among themselves, elicit ideas and discuss the differences.

1.5 The aim of this activity is to consolidate students' understanding that writing in examinations is still a process, but is a shorter one than normal essay assignments.

Answers:

Stage in the process	Writing essays in examinations	Course assignments
Analyzing the title	✓	✓
Brainstorming ideas	✓	✓
Organizing your ideas/plan	✓	✓
Self-evaluation		✓
Peer evaluation		✓
Writing a first draft	✓	✓
Self-evaluation	✓	✓
Peer evaluation		✓
Revising your draft	✓	✓
Writing a second draft		✓
Teacher evaluation/feedback		✓
Evaluation of teacher feedback		✓
Revising your second draft		✓
Writing a third draft		✓
Writing a final draft		✓

1.7 This activity revisits the skill, already practised in previous units, of analyzing essay questions. You may wish to look at only three or four of the questions, according to the level and interests of the class. You could divide the class into groups to look at different questions. You may choose to analyze the questions together as a class so that you can gloss any difficult vocabulary.

This is an appropriate moment to look at the list of essay words (a–t) on page 31 of the Course Book, and discuss what each word is asking the writer to do. In Task 3, students will be asked to do the activity to match these words with their meanings.

Focus of the questions:
1   **a)** What properties of microorganisms cause food spoilage? Why do they cause food spoilage, and why are they major causes (including what are other causes)?
    b) What is food spoilage and how do microbes cause food spoilage?
    c) Different methods of reducing or preventing food spoilage.

2 Answer should focus on why and how livestock contribute to the welfare of the poorest people in developing countries.

3 Answer should focus on definitions of breed, breed substitution, crossbreeding and within-breed selection; examples should be given of how these cause genetic change.

4 Answer requires a comparison and contrast of the different feed resources for ruminants and non-ruminants. Evaluate these resources in order to answer the second part of the question.

5 Answer should include definitions of free trade and international economic growth, and an examination of whether international economic growth is a consequence of free trade.

6 Answer requires definitions of international aid and global development and an analysis of whether global development can only take place if international aid exists.

7 Answer requires an explanation of the nature and structure of north–south relations, and whether such a structure has a negative effect on the development of less-developed countries.

8 Answer requires concise explanations in response to a), b), c).

9 Answer requires a description of the techniques, how they work and an evaluation of their effectiveness.

10 Answer requires a discussion of the impact of global warming on the ecology of the world, and what this means for the future.

11 Answer requires a description of the problems, possible causes of the problems and an evaluation of the use of subsurface drainage.

Text 3b | Telemedicine comes home

Task 2: Writing your essay

2.1 It is worth spending some time discussing with students how they might approach this question. It asks students to describe the potential benefits of telemedicine in preventing and curing disease, and to discuss whether more potential applications will be found in preventing disease than curing it.

2.3 Text 3b in the Source Book (pages 22–24) is to stimulate ideas, although some lower-level groups may find it challenging.

Remind students to read through the key writing skills section on answering examination questions before they begin their plan.

Task 3: Key words used in examination questions

This is a surprisingly difficult activity so students should work in groups. When they have done as much as they can, provide them with photocopies of the answer sheet on page 47 or display an OHT.

Answers:
1i, 2o, 3a, 4f, 5q, 6m, 7j, 8d, 9s, 10b, 11g,
12k, 13t, 14r, 15c, 16n, 17p, 18e, 19h, 20l

Giving feedback on timed writing
A suggested marking scheme is given on pages 50–51 of this Teacher's Book. It consists of a set of criteria at different levels, and boxes representing the appropriate criteria for the essay can be ticked. This will give students an idea of their strengths and weaknesses when writing in timed conditions. The criteria are divided into the following categories:
- appropriate incorporation of relevant content;
- developing a clear line of argument and organizing ideas coherently;
- stance/position of writer, i.e., the viewpoint that the writer takes on the topic;
- range and appropriate use of vocabulary and grammar;
- accuracy of grammar use;
- communicative quality.

Typically, a student who consistently achieves A grades for each criterion would be ready to study a linguistically demanding subject, such as economics or politics. A student who is between A and B would be ready to study a less linguistically demanding subject, such as computer science or construction management.

You may also wish to give more detailed comment on the student scripts and ask for a second draft.

There are two further timed writing tasks on the following pages that you can photocopy and give your students as appropriate during the course.

Unit summary

1   **Sample answers:**
    a) You still have to analyze the title, brainstorm ideas, organize ideas, write a first draft, self-evaluate, revise first draft – and finally get it marked (teacher feedback).
    b) Edit the first draft and add any information that could improve the answer.
    c) Key words
    d) A thesis statement
    e) Clarity of ideas, spelling and grammar

2   There are so many permutations of these that it would be useful to discuss answers with the students and clarify the most appropriate answers.

    Possible answers:
    a) analyze, comment on, discuss, evaluate/consider, evaluate, identify, outline
    b) consider, compare, discuss, evaluate, identify, outline, summarize, (state)
    c) analyze, consider, define, describe, discuss, identify, outline/comment on, compare, contrast, evaluate

Web resources

Writing essays for exams: The owl at Purdue
The owl at Purdue is an American on-line writing lab which covers all aspects of academic writing. This page gives an overview of how to write an effective exam essay, and lists some useful language for exam essays.
http://owl.english.purdue.edu/owl/resource/737/01/

CILL: Explanation of key words in essays
Comprehensive list of verbs that are commonly used in essay titles together with example titles and links to dictionary definitions of the key words.
http://elc.polyu.edu.hk/cill/eap/functionsexplanation.htm

Photocopiable handout

a	account	**1**	**i**	give an explanation of something in detail (what it is like, how it works, etc.)
b	analyze	**2**	**o**	give the main ideas
c	apply (to)	**3**	**a**	a) e.g., give an account of/a brief account of – describe b) e.g., account for – give the reasons for
d	comment (on)	**4**	**f**	describe and say what you think about something
e	compare	**5**	**q**	show the connection between two or more things
f	consider	**6**	**m**	describe items that belong to a particular group/category
g	contrast	**7**	**j**	write in detail about all the different aspects of an issue or statement, including reasons for a particular viewpoint (give your own viewpoint or evidence that you have thought about a topic)
h	define	**8**	**d**	give your views on something, say what you think about something; it is often used with a quotation, with which you should agree or disagree
i	describe	**9**	**s**	give evidence to strengthen your point
j	discuss	**10**	**b**	consider very carefully/examine to find out what something consists of
k	evaluate	**11**	**g**	describe the main aspects of two or more things to show their differences
l	explain	**12**	**k**	write about something in detail from the point of view of its strengths and weaknesses, advantages and disadvantages, and importance
m	identify	**13**	**t**	say clearly
n	illustrate	**14**	**r**	write the main points of a topic
o	outline	**15**	**c**	put something to use, show how something (e.g., a theory, certain findings, data, research results) can be used in a particular situation
p	prove	**16**	**n**	include many examples
q	relate	**17**	**p**	show that something is true
r	summarize	**18**	**e**	describe the main aspects of two or more things to show their similarities
s	support	**19**	**h**	give an explanation of the meaning of a term
t	state	**20**	**l**	write to express the issue or idea clearly; a) explain why – give the reason for, cause of something, b) explain how – describe (a process) clearly

Timed writing 2

Write an essay on the following topic:

The impact of on-screen violence is having a serious social effect on young people. Discuss.

You should try to write 300–400 words.
You may make notes here:

_____

_____

_____

_____

_____

_____

_____

_____

_____

_____

_____

_____

_____

_____

_____

_____

Timed writing 3

Write an essay on the following topic:

Traditional values in society are in danger of completely disappearing as a result of modern developments. Discuss.

You should try to write 300–400 words.
You may make notes here:

_____

_____

_____

_____

_____

_____

_____

_____

_____

_____

_____

_____

_____

_____

_____

_____

_____

Timed writing grades

Name: _____

Essay: _____

A+	
All your main points are relevant. One or two of your minor points may be irrelevant. You have used the content very appropriately.	
You have organized your ideas and developed your argument clearly, coherently and logically.	
Your thesis communicates your position clearly and is well presented and maintained, and sophisticated in places.	
You have used a wide range of vocabulary and grammatical structure with good control.	
You have made only one or two errors in grammar use, which do not interfere with comprehension.	
Your writing communicates your message fluently.	

A	
All your main points are relevant. Only a few of your minor points may be irrelevant. You have used the content appropriately, for the most part.	
You have organized your ideas and developed your argument mainly clearly, coherently and logically.	
Your thesis communicates your position to the reader clearly, and is well presented and maintained.	
You have used a wide range of vocabulary and grammatical structure with reasonable control.	
You have made only minor errors in grammar use, which do not interfere with comprehension.	
Your writing causes your reader few difficulties.	

B	
Most of your main points are relevant. Some of your minor points may be irrelevant. Some of your main and supporting points may be confused. You may have used the content inappropriately, and you may not have sufficient content.	
Overall, you have organized your ideas well, coherently and clearly, but in some places your argument needs further development.	
Your thesis communicates your position to the reader, but this is not sufficiently well maintained throughout the essay.	

Photocopiable

You have <u>either</u> been ambitious and used a fairly wide range of vocabulary and grammatical structure in your writing, which in some places needs further control, <u>or</u> you have used a limited range of vocabulary and grammatical structure well.	
There are some errors in your grammar use, which may very occasionally interfere with comprehension.	
Your writing communicates satisfactorily; there is some fluency.	

C	
Many of your main points are not relevant, and many of your points require further support with details. Your main and supporting points are sometimes confused.	
There is some evidence of coherent organization of ideas in your writing, but there needs to be further development of your argument.	
You have tried to communicate a thesis to the reader, but this is difficult to follow.	
A reasonable range of vocabulary and grammatical structure in your writing is evident, but more control is needed.	
There are frequent errors in your use of grammar, which sometimes interfere with comprehension.	
Your writing communicates, although there is some strain for the reader.	

D	
It is difficult to identify your main points, and most of them are not supported.	
There is little evidence of any coherent organization of ideas or development of argument.	
It is difficult to identify a thesis which communicates your position to the reader at any point in the essay.	
A limited range of vocabulary and grammatical structure is evident in your writing, but a lot more control is needed.	
There are many errors in your use of grammar, which often interfere with comprehension.	
Your writing communicates, but requires effort by the reader.	

E	
There are few ideas, which are undeveloped, in your essay.	
There is very little evidence of coherent organization of ideas and development of argument in your writing.	
There is no attempt at a thesis which communicates your position to the reader.	
The range of vocabulary and grammatical structure used in your essay is very limited, with little control.	
There are very many errors in your use of grammar, most of which interfere with comprehension.	
Your writing communicates, but requires substantial effort by the reader.	

Teacher: _____

4 Statistics without tears

This unit will help students:
- make decisions about what the essay title is asking them to do, and organize their ideas;
- consider what information in a text is useful to support their ideas, and how to incorporate that in their own writing;
- learn how to end a paragraph with an effective concluding sentence;
- practise effectively ending an essay with a conclusion.

This unit will prepare the students to write an essay on the following topic:
Statistics should be interpreted with caution as they can be misleading; they can both lie and tell the truth. Discuss.

Text 4 | Statistics without tears

Task 1: Microskills: Organizing your ideas

The essay is another discursive/argumentative type of essay, to give students further practice in writing to persuade their audience of their viewpoint, a necessary skill in academic life.

1.1 Students should come up with *statistics*, *interpreted*, *caution*, *misleading*, *lie* and *truth*.

1.3 Students should come up with ideas relating to what the essay is asking them to do:
- describe the different ways statistics can be interpreted;
- say how they can be misleading;
- give examples of situations when statistics are made to lie and when they are made to tell the truth.

It is important to stress that they can use knowledge of their own subject area to support their ideas.

1.5 Elicit different ways to organize ideas from the students, e.g., the different uses of statistics, how they can be interpreted to lie, how they can be interpreted to tell the truth – both with examples – and an evaluation of both interpretations.

1.6 The aim of this activity is to develop awareness of how statistics can be made to tell two different stories, to assist students to generate ideas for their essays. Tell the students to read Texts 4-1, 4-2 and 4-3 in the Source Book (pages 25–33, entitled *Statistics without tears*).

1.7 Tell the students to read the article *Surge in violence, or just a quirk?* and identify the main message of the article.

The main message is that although the surge in offences classified as 'most serious violence against the person' can be explained by the recent reclassification, the lack of faith in the government's use of statistics means that it has simply led to an undermining of balanced discussion.

It is useful at this point to ask students to bring in their own material showing how statistics can be manipulated. They can bring articles from their own subject area or general subject areas. In the next class, this can be exploited by having the students explain their articles and their meaning to others in small groups.

1.8 The aim of this activity is to heighten awareness of the situations in which statistics can be twisted. You will probably need to explain the word *manipulated*.

1.9 The aim of this activity is to look at statistics from the point of view of those who make use of them, sometimes representing the truth and sometimes not, sometimes appropriately and sometimes not. Among those who produce statistics you could include governments, companies, academics and researchers.

1.10/1.11 Point out that not all answers are clear from the chart. The questions are just to stimulate discussion. For example, although they come from the National Statistics website, they were compiled by the Office for National Statistics.

Answers:
a) a decline in crime
b) society is becoming safer
c) Office for National Statistics
d) presumably the police
e) the government, the police and the public could all benefit in some way
f) government: could show their policies are working; police: could show they are doing a good job; public: could reassure and make them feel safer

1.12 It is useful to have a plenary and share students' ideas, as some of them may find it difficult to think of specific situations.

Task 2: Writing your essay

2.1 Having done a lot of input and groundwork on the planning stage, the students should not need too much guidance in their planning, although as it can be a difficult topic for some students, it is worth monitoring this stage carefully.

2.2 Students should now be familiar with the peer evaluation process and you should not need to monitor this so carefully.

Task 3: Microskills: Concluding sentences

3.1 Lower-level students may need to be reminded that, to complete the task, it is not necessary to stop and check each word they do not know; the main focus needs to be on the last sentence. However, for the third paragraph you may want to gloss the word *demographic* (connected to the scientific study of population numbers).

1 The last sentence is a conclusion, or deduction, of the previous information.
2 The last sentence acts as a transition between the introductory paragraph and the following information in the chapter.
3 The last sentence predicts possible future consequences of rapid population growth.
4 The last sentence makes a conclusion from the information given in the paragraph.

3.3 The students may come up with the following suggestions, as well as some of their own.

Summary:
The concluding sentence in a paragraph can:
- summarize the main ideas of your paragraph;
- restate the main topic;
- make a conclusion from the information given in the paragraph;

- predict the future;
- suggest possible solutions;
- link the ideas of the paragraph to the ideas of the following paragraph.

3.4 Point out that individual concluding sentences can have more than one function. The main functions of concluding sentences in Ex 3.1 are:

1 make a conclusion;
2 link ideas to the following paragraph;
3 predict the future;
4 make a conclusion.

3.5 Students will come up with a number of variations for a suitable concluding sentence, but here are some possibilities:

1
- Thus, global warming has caused much damage. (*summary*)
- Thus, action should be taken to stop the damage that is being caused by global warming. (*suggestion*)
- If action is not taken to slow down this process, then by the year 2050 the Earth will be a completely different environment. (*prediction*)

2
- Unless action is taken by the government to improve the situation, the quality of teaching will continue to deteriorate. (*prediction*)
- It is therefore suggested that the government takes appropriate action to improve the situation. (*suggestion*)

3
- Thus, changes in working habits are due to progress in technological development. (*conclusion of information in the paragraph*)
- However, progress in technological development can also lead to negative consequences. (*transition to next paragraph about negative consequences*)

Task 4: Microskills: Conclusions

4.1 Be open to students' suggestions, but as a guide, the following points are important when thinking about the function of a conclusion:
- a summary of the main ideas;
- a conclusion that can be drawn from the information in the essay;
- a prediction of future events.

Remind students that no new information should be given in the conclusion, only a discussion of what has already been said.

4.3 You may wish to begin by showing the conclusion on page 58. This is an example of a rather poor conclusion from a student so has not been included in the Course Book. A possible rewrite has also been given. Points you may wish to make:
- It is a conclusion drawing on information from the essay.
- It is generally not good practice to begin, *To conclude* or *In conclusion*.
- The conclusion is not expressed with any force or clarity.

Possible rewrite:
Because of the difficult circumstances in which many people in developing countries live, many are searching for an ideal as represented by life in more developed countries. They are aware that an improvement in living standards would not be impossible to achieve if it was not for the issues discussed above, such as outside interference, unfair debt problems and inappropriate institutions of government. Despite an awareness of these issues and, in particular, the destabilizing influence of power and money, there is an optimism that this will one day no longer pose an obstacle to the fulfilment of their dreams.

Here are some suggestions as to what these conclusions are trying to do:
1   A conclusion of information in the essay and a suggestion about what should be done.
2   A summary of the main body and a suggestion of what should be done.
3   A summary of the main body and a prediction of what might happen if things do not change.

4.4   The correct order is 2), 3), 1).

4.5   The correct order is 3), 1), 4), 2).

Unit summary

1   Although much of this table is easy to complete, students will nevertheless have to think carefully about some aspects. Encourage them to see this as an opportunity to reflect on what they have done and prepare for Ex 2.

2   **Answers:**
    1.1–1.4, 1.5–1.7, 1.8–1.10, Task 2, Task 3, Task 4

Web resources

Econoclass: statistics can be misleading
This site encourages students to look at a range of authentic US statistics in graphs, charts and news articles, and work out why they are misleading.
http://www.econoclass.com/misleadingstats.html

Writing machine - conclusions
This section of the Hong Kong University website gives advice for writing conclusions to academic essays. Students can also read and evaluate examples of good and bad conclusions.
http://ec.hku.hk/acadgrammar/essay/section4/four.htm

University of Essex: My skills: introduction and conclusion writing
This page from the academic skills site of the University of Essex recaps on introductions and conclusions, and gives additional information and advice. It also includes four awareness-raising tasks.
http://www.essex.ac.uk/myskills/skills/writing/introConclWriting.asp#02tasks.

Summary:

The concluding sentence in a paragraph can:

- summarize the main ideas of your paragraph;
- restate the main topic;
- make a conclusion from the information given in the paragraph;
- predict the future;
- suggest possible solutions;
- link the ideas of the paragraph to the ideas of the following paragraph.

Photocopiable

To conclude, searching for an ideal world is the main thought that occupies the minds of most people in developing countries, because they are living in such a difficult situation compared with the developed countries. These people know that it would not be an impossible achievement, if there were no debts and no unfair constitutions with no interference in their internal problems. They consider that there will be a day when money and power will not be considered the most important aspects of life.

Possible rewrite
Because of the difficult circumstances in which many people in developing countries live, many are searching for an ideal as represented by life in more developed countries. They are aware that an improvement in living standards would not be impossible to achieve if it were not for the issues discussed above, such as outside interference, unfair debt problems and inappropriate institutions of government. Despite an awareness of these issues and, in particular, the destabilizing influence of power and money, there is an optimism that these current difficulties will one day no longer pose an obstacle to the fulfilment of their dreams.

5 Human activity and climate change

This unit will help students:
- practise writing clear definitions;
- learn how to support and develop their ideas.

This unit will prepare the students to write an essay on the following topic:
What role has human activity played in causing climate change?

<table>
<tr><td>**Text 5**</td><td>Human activity and climate change</td></tr>
</table>

Tell the students to read Texts 5-1 to 5-4 on *Human activities and climate change* in the Source Book, pages 34–41. By now, the students should be more independent in the planning stage of writing. You may want to check how far they have got with their plans to ensure that they are on track. Students are expected to employ the skills that are developed in this writing unit when writing their essay. They will be evaluated at the peer evaluation stage.

Task 1: Microskills: Short definitions

1.1 Students should be able to point out that the verb *teaches* is only a different form of the word that is being defined, *teacher*. Thus, it is not a suitable definition, since if the reader does not know the word *teacher*, s/he will not know the verb *teaches*.

1.2 It is common to define a word in the following cases:
1 when there are a number of possible definitions of a word and the writer wants to clarify which one s/he is referring to;
2 when a writer is writing for a readership outside her/his subject area. It would be worth pointing out that when a writer is writing for her/his own community of scholars, there are generally common views about certain terms, which therefore do not need defining.

1.3 **Answers:**
a) no **b)** yes **c)** yes **d)** yes
e) no **f)** yes **g)** no **h)** yes

1.5 This would be an appropriate moment to revise the sort of language that is used when writing definitions. It is important to emphasize:
1 that it is more appropriate to use *may be defined as* rather than *is*; by doing this, the writer is acknowledging that there are other possible definitions of the same word;
2 the use of the relative pronoun.

1.6 For all the examples, *may be defined as* is substituted for *is* and *are*.

Formal definitions:
It is worth spending time explaining how to write a formal definition and giving the students some practice. They will need the ability to write accurate definitions on their courses.

1.7 **Answers:**
Formal definitions:
a) A square may be defined as a geometric figure which has four straight sides and four right angles.

b) A television may be defined as a system for reproducing an actual or recorded scene at a distance on a screen by radio transmission, usually with appropriate sounds. (*adapted from OED*)

c) A dictionary may be defined as a book which deals with the individual words of a language, giving their meaning, pronunciation and use; the words are arranged in alphabetical order.

Naming definitions:
Compare with formal definitions and make sure the students are able to do Ex 1.8–1.10.

1.8 Answers:
Naming definitions:

a) A geometric figure which has four straight sides and four right angles may be called a square.

b) A system for reproducing an actual or recorded scene at a distance on a screen by radio transmission, usually with appropriate sounds, may be called a television. (*adapted from OED*)

c) A book which deals with the individual words of a language, giving their meaning, pronunciation and use, and in which the words are arranged in alphabetical order, may be called a dictionary.

Students may, of course, come up with suitably worded alternative definitions.

1.9 Answers:
1 Naming
2 Formal
3 Naming
4 Formal

1.10 See the Source Book page 35, lines 7–8 (formal definition of *climate*) and lines 18–21 (naming definition of *the greenhouse effect*).

Remind the students that definitions may occur at the beginning of a text, in the first few paragraphs.

Task 2: Extended definitions

2.1 The students will probably need prompting to come up with ideas. You could give one example and get them to discuss in pairs to come up with more. You might want to look at the first extract in Ex 2.2 to elicit how it is done there (using an example) before discussing further ideas.

A definition can be extended by giving:
- examples;
- further details;
- more specific detail about general information already given in the simple definition;
- further definitions of words used in the simple definition;
- advantages or disadvantages of an aspect of the 'thing' being defined.

2.2 1 This paragraph has been extended with an example. Note the use of *refers*.

2 This paragraph has been extended with specific information about governmental loans; that is, the difference between them and commercial loans. There is also an indication of one of the positive aspects.

2.3 Point out the value of being able to define your area of study.

Answers:
a) Anthropology and physics
b) Subjects are becoming more specific

2.4 This definition has been extended by using further definitions of an important word in the simple definition, as well as a list of the topics covered by psychology. As it then goes on to explain the first of these topics in more detail, we can assume that it will continue with an explanation of the rest of the topics.

2.5 Students write a definition of their subject.

2.6 It might be useful to discuss this first as a class.

Task 3: Microskills: Exemplification and support

3.1 The reader should be satisfied with 2), but not 1), for the following reasons:

1 In this paragraph, the writer has assumed that the reader knows about the discrimination faced by the *burakumin* as a result of traditionally having had the 'dirty' jobs like slaughterer and gravedigger; there is a jump to the idea that they face problems, but no reason is given.

The writer needs to introduce the idea of discrimination clearly and expand on it.

In both of the above cases, the reader is left asking the questions *Why? How?* etc.

Remind students that if the reader is left asking questions, then the writer has not put in enough information – the ideas have not been developed enough. The writer cannot assume that the reader makes the same connections as the writer has made, as the writer has spent much more time thinking about the topic.

2 In this paragraph, the writer has given the reader much more explanation to expand her/his main idea. S/he extends her/his idea in the second sentence, and then gives an example which s/he further extends, and gives other reasons for the conflict.

3.3 **1** In this paragraph, the writer has picked up on the main idea in the first sentence, that of *a series of ... changes*. S/he then proceeds to explain examples of these changes, using the signposts *First and foremost* and *Second*. The first example is mainly a description of what happened, whereas in the second, the writer goes further by giving reasons for the change plus extra detail.

The main point students need to understand here is the use of *first, second*, etc. (chronological markers), and the more detailed explanation. You may also wish to point out the difference between *first* and *firstly*, and that strictly speaking the writer should have used *firstly* and *secondly* here.

2 In this paragraph, the writer has used statistical data or fact to give more details of the population. S/he has also given reasons for a particular situation.

3.4 Students should come up with ideas such as: by using examples, using statistical fact, using chronological listing and giving reasons.

3.5 **Answers:**
The sentence from Ex 3.1, 2 is the writer's opinion.
The sentence from Ex 3.3, 2 is fact.

3.7 Students should come up with expressions like:
- *an (a good) illustration of this*
- *an example of this can be seen in*
- *for example*
- *for instance*
- *a case in point*
- *such as*

Make sure that the students have the full list as they will need it to complete the next task.

3.8 **Answers:**
1 *a case in point*
2 *for instance*
3 *for example*
4 *such as*
5 *a good illustration of this*

3.9 It is expected that students will use chronological listing to develop this paragraph.

3.10 It is expected that students will continue the paragraph by describing the different types of expenditure of single males and females, and include some figures from the table. They should also attempt an explanation of the differences.

You may wish to spend some time eliciting relevant content for this paragraph.

Task 4: Writing your essay

4.1 Elicit from students how they will improve their essays with definitions and support for their ideas.

4.3 The peer evaluation sheet includes questions reflecting the microskills covered in this unit, as well as the general ones on organization and structure.

Unit summary

1   As this was encouraging students to use their own voice (for explaining to another student), it was felt best not to have sample answers.

2   **Answers:**
    a) Introducing a chronological marker
    b) Introducing statistical facts
    c) Introducing examples
    d) Introducing a supporting fact

Web resources

Language and learning online: Defining your topic
A summary of how to use definitions (formal/informal and expanded definitions), together with examples.
http://www.monash.edu.au/lls/llonline/writing/general/thesis-edit/2.2.xml

BBC Learning English: Talk about English: climate change
The BBC world service programmes for learners of English have several programmes which discuss the issues and language connected with climate change. There are two links here:

This webcast is an audio discussion that examines key issues.
http://www.bbc.co.uk/worldservice/learningenglish/webcast/070426_climate_change/

This site explains vocabulary in the news connected with climate change.
http://www.bbc.co.uk/worldservice/learningenglish/newsenglish/witn/2004/12/041210_climate.shtml

6 The global village

This unit will help students:
- learn how to choose appropriate patterns of organizing the content of their essays;
- practise incorporating ideas from their reading into their writing.

This unit will prepare the students to write an essay on the following topic:
Discuss the positive and negative effects of globalization on the world today.

Task 1: Microskills: Organizing essays of cause and effect

The aim of this task is to raise students' awareness of various ways of organizing an essay of this type.

Point out that two lines have been provided for each answer in case the students wish to elaborate in their answers as in some of the answers below.

1.1 **Answers:**

Para 1:   introduction to topic (general to specific)
Para 2:   situation (patterns of holiday-making)
Para 3:   effects of tourism (problems)
Para 4:   effects of tourism on environment
Para 5:   effects on government (action to oppose the threat of tourism)
Para 6:   evaluation of action
Para 7:   conclusion/summary of main body

1.2 There are two main points to elicit here:
- The writer has only really addressed part of the question; s/he has not discussed the positive effects, thus the essay is not equally balanced.
- Some students may say that the writer did not need to discuss the solutions in such detail. However, as the task has the word *discuss* in it, an analysis of the problems and possible solutions shows a higher-level approach to the task.

1.3 When discussing the ways a cause-and-effect essay can be developed, it is important to emphasize that the two ways presented in the Course Book are only to give students an idea of *possible* approaches; eventually, they will be able to be more flexible in their approach. Providing initial help by introducing these possible structures will encourage weaker students to be more confident in their approach.

- Point out that the cause section and the effect section in pattern 1 can be *more* than three paragraphs each, depending on their specific topic.
- Similarly, the cause/effect paragraphs in pattern 2 can be more in number.

Answers:
a) The essay seems to follow the second pattern more closely.
b) The choice of which pattern of organization to use depends on the topic of the writing. The second pattern is more useful when the causes and effects are very closely connected, whereas the first pattern is more useful when there is not such a close link.

1.5 This task raises awareness of suitable connectors for cause and effect. Begin by eliciting the purpose of the phrases (introducing cause and effect) and the grammar of each item. *A consequence of …* and *Owing to …* are both compound prepositions and *This has caused* is a straightforward use of subject + verb.

Elicit other ideas for suitable connectors and write them on the board. You may need to prompt them to come up with variations on the compound prepositions such as *due to* and *because of,* and different verbs such as *result in.* You may also want to prompt them to come up with the use of the conditional.

Elicit the other connector in paragraph 1, *resulting in,* and then let the students find the others in paragraphs 3–7.

Answers:

Para 3:   *have caused* (line 1), *result of* (line 3), *at the expense of* (line 5), *due to* (line 8)
Para 4:   *effect of* (line 1), *it causes* (line 1), *because of* (line 4), *created by* (line 7), *has caused* (line 8), *gives rise to* (line 8), *causes* (line 9), *has resulted in* (line 11)
Para 5:   *has prompted* (line 1)
Para 6:   *is still causing* (line 3), *because of* (line 6),
Para 7:   *If nothing is done* (line 6)

1.6   Go through the language to express cause and effect on pages 59–60 of the Course Book, drawing attention to the sentence structure.

If short of time, this can be set for homework. You may wish to give your students further practice in using cause-and-effect expressions.

Text 6   The global village

Task 2: Writing your essay

By now, students should be much more independent in their approach to essay writing and in the choices that they need to make to respond to the task.

Tell the students to read the text *The global village* in the Source Book, pages 42–55, as part of their preparation.

Unit summary

1 Encourage the students to discuss these points in pairs or groups outside the class.

2 These answers, although fairly obvious, highlight some important issues.

Answers:
a) the topic of your essay
b) function
c) should try to
d) more flexible
e) clearer and easier to follow

Web resources

VLC Academic Writer: Language
These pages will help students with useful chunks of language to help structure their essays. They are divided into essential language and advanced language sections and list conventional phrases and expressions according to function, e.g., cause and effect, comparison, analogy, etc., as well as language for giving your opinion, point of view, limiting the scope, etc.
http:vlc.polyu.edu.hk/AcademicWriter/Frames/framesLanguage.htm

University of Essex: My Skills: Essay structure
Pages that clarify different ways of structuring your arguments in an essay. These include: the horizontal structure used in cause and effect essays, and the vertical structure of problem–solutions–implications–evaluation essays.
http://www.essex.ac.uk/myskills/skills/writing/essayStructure.asp#04

7 The new linguistic order

This unit will help students:
- learn how to choose appropriate patterns of organizing the content of their essays;
- further practise incorporating ideas from their reading into their writing.

This unit will prepare students to write an essay based on the topics of either *globalization* or *the rise of English as a world language*.

This unit gives students the opportunity to develop their awareness of patterns of organization by practising a pattern of *Situation–Problems–Solutions–Implications–Evaluation*. They should use information from both texts, and any of their own texts, to support the ideas in their essays.

Task 1: Microskills: Organizing essays: Situation, problems, solutions, implications, evaluation

1.1 Go through the introduction and explain how the organization pattern shown in the box has been applied in the student text. Highlight the fact that this organization can be used for any length of text, from a paragraph to a complete book.

1.2 You may need to encourage the students to think of an appropriate situation, using pair or group discussion.

1.3 Ask the students to read the text and to think about these questions:
- What is the problem?
- What is the solution?
- What are the implications of the solution?

1.4 Answer:

Situation: increase in movement of populations across borders

Problem(s): a global migration crisis; ethical issues, e.g., proportion of ethnic groups in a country, national identity of a country, racism, the effect of a multicultural society and the distribution of wealth

Solution(s): establishment of language programmes, cultural exchange and awareness-raising programmes, and employment opportunities; more open-mindedness

Implication(s): higher level of cooperation between host country and the country of migrants' origin; more cooperation at levels of citizens, ethnic groups and political bodies; it will take time

Evaluation: with time and with greater understanding of the global picture and a possible fair governing body, the problems resulting from the issues of global migration will be minimized

1.6 *A further problem might be:*
The organizational problems and financial implications related to greater cooperation; also the resistance of some governments to cooperate.

Further solution:
The creation of organizations to implement new measures and to coordinate meetings.

Further implications/evaluation:
There will be further economic and social problems before this can be done. Financial aid will probably have to be obtained from the taxpayer.

If you feel that your students need further practice in approaching a problem in this way, you could ask them to think of a situation in their own country which has led to problems. Students write two short paragraphs and exchange these with a partner. They then complete a *Situation–Problems–Solutions–Implications–Evaluation* flow chart summarizing the content of the paragraphs.

1.7 The aim of this question is to raise students' awareness of appropriate language structures for evaluation.

Elicit the following:
- conditionals, e.g., *If X is done, then Y will happen.*
- *should*, e.g., *This solution should be effective in that it will ...*
- use of modals and hedging, e.g., *This may lead to ...*

Text 7 | The new linguistic order

Task 2: Writing your essay

The aim of this task is to encourage students' ability to respond to tasks independently, and to make considered choices about their reading and writing. Students should now be able to carry out question analysis and associated purposeful reading accordingly.

Tell the students to read Text 7-1 in the Source Book (pages 56–64, entitled *The new linguistic order*) as preparation. It will also be useful if they reread the text entitled *The global village* from Unit 6.

Students have a choice of essay in this unit. They should be encouraged to use an *S-P-S-I-E* pattern. However, you may want to enter into a discussion about the fact that many texts are a combination of patterns and that they could also have sections of their essays that have a cause-and-effect pattern, or a comparison/contrast pattern.

As this is the last essay of the course, students are being challenged to refer to two sources. You may need to make the link between the two texts more explicit for some students, i.e., that the spread of English is both a cause and a consequence of globalization. If you have a very able group, you may like to challenge them further by finding a third relevant text, or asking them to find one in the library.

2.6 There is no peer evaluation sheet for this unit, as by now students should be able to approach this activity without prompts.

Unit summary

You may wish the students to think about and discuss these questions in preparation for a class discussion prior to completing the final course summary.

Web resources

BBC Learning English: English and the future
Online article by linguist David Graddol, together with discussion contributions from English students from all over the world.
http://www.bbc.co.uk/worldservice/learningenglish/radio/specials/1720_ten_years/page9.shtml

University of Birmingham: English for International students: Kibbitzers
Kibbitzers is a reference to people who observe and discuss chess problems, but here it refers to discussion of errors in students' work. The site lists common language and vocabulary errors and gives examples of problems and corrections from students' actual essays.
http://www.eisu.bham.ac.uk/support/online/kibbitzers.shtml

University of Richmond: Writing web
This site is complex in places, but it has some interesting and innovative ideas on how to approach different stages in the writing process, including editing and peer-editing. Students can explore the topics by looking at the writer's web mind map and clicking on the area that interests them.
http://writing2.richmond.edu/writing/wweb.html

Situation: increase in movement of populations across borders

Problem(s): a global migration crisis; ethical issues, e.g., proportion of ethnic groups in a country, national identity of a country, racism, the effect of a multicultural society and the distribution of wealth

Solution(s): establishment of language programmes, cultural exchange and awareness-raising programmes, and employment opportunities; more open-mindedness

Implication(s): higher level of cooperation between host country and the country of migrants' origin; more cooperation at levels of citizens, ethnic groups and political bodies; it will take time

Evaluation: with time and with greater understanding of the global picture and a possible fair governing body, the problems resulting from the issues of global migration will be minimized

a Appendices

Appendix 1   **Questions and glossary for Unit 4, Ex 1.7**

The comprehension questions in Appendix 1 of the course book are designed as an additional activity for use by weaker students.

Appendix 2   **(Course Book):Organizing essays of comparison and contrast**

The supplementary unit in Appendix 2 of the Course Book can be used during the course to show how essays of comparison and contrast can be structured. It can be stand-alone or it can be integrated with writing an essay. An example might be:

Compare and contrast the education system in England with that of your own country.

Appendix 3   **(Course Book): Assessing my progress**

The aim of the activity in Appendix 3 of the Course Book is to encourage students to assess their progress in academic writing over the course. They should try to identify consistent patterns of strengths and weaknesses, as well as identifying areas where they have improved.

Some students may find this difficult to do at first, so you may need to give them some concrete examples of how to do this.

Students should fill in the table on page 79 of their books.

At the end, have a plenary session in which each student states one or two areas that s/he is going to work on in the future to improve their writing.

This self-assessment can be done at a certain stage during the course or at the end.